CW00502427

CREDIT REPAIR

Stop Being Humiliated By Banks With The Ultimate
Guide To Repairing Your Credit And Boosting Your
Credit Score

ANDREW BENNET

© Copyright 2021 Andrew Bennet - All rights reserved.

The content contained within this book may not be reproduced, duplicated or transmitted without direct written permission from the author or the publisher. Under no circumstances will any blame or legal responsibility be held against the publisher, or author, for any damages, reparation, or monetary loss due to the information contained within this book. Either directly or indirectly.

Legal Notice:

This book is copyright protected. This book is only for personal use. You cannot amend, distribute, sell, use, quote or paraphrase any part, or the content within this book, without the consent of the author or publisher.

Disclaimer Notice:

Please note the information contained within this document is for educational and entertainment purposes only. All effort has been executed to present accurate, up to date, and reliable, complete information. No warranties of any kind are declared or implied. Readers acknowledge that the author is not engaging in the rendering of legal, financial, medical or professional advice. The content within this book has been derived from various sources. Please consult a licensed professional before attempting any techniques outlined in this book.

By reading this document, the reader agrees that under no circumstances is the author responsible for any losses, direct or indirect, which are incurred as a result of the use of information contained within this document, including, but not limited to, — errors, omissions, or inaccuracies.

Chapter 1.   Increase Credit Limit

One of the least utilized strategies for lowering your debt utilization is a credit limit increase.

All you need to do is call your lender and ask if a credit limit increase is available for your account. Most people don't know that a customer service representative will pull up your entire account before they even answer the phone. They use caller ID to identify you, then have you prove your identity. Once proven, they have all your past conversations, your limits, balances, and possible upgrades available.

They just won't tell you unless you ask. By requesting a credit limit increase you're effectively increasing your available credit without increasing your balance.

For example, if you have one card with a $500 limit and $250 balance, then you're at 50% utilization.

If you get a $500 limit increase, then you have $1000 limit with a $250 balance. That brings your utilization down to only 25% instantly!

The lower your utilization, the higher your scores. With a secured card you simply increase your deposit.

For a regular credit card, make sure you make timely payments for at least 6 months, though 9 months is better. Make sure you keep your card under 50% utilization on all your cards. They won't approve you if you're maxed out or have missed payments within the past year. If they ask you what you're going to use the money for, don't say gambling, or anything irresponsible.

Say you're trying to improve your FICO scores or that you just got a raise and wanted to buy some new furniture. If they ask how large an increase you would like, ask them how much you qualify for. They can tell you after a minute or so.

If you're approved, then you just raised your credit scores with a phone call.

Become an Authorized User

A very simple yet effective technique for boosting your credit scores it to "piggyback" on someone else's credit history and become an Authorized User (AU) on their account.

An AU account is not like a Joint Account.

With a Joint Account both you and the primary holder can add to the credit balance, but you're also both liable for the debts.

If, for example, the primary files for bankruptcy protection, then you will be on the hook for the full balance.

You should avoid Joint accounts at all costs.

With an Authorized User account, only the primary card holder is liable for the debt.

However, the trade line appears on BOTH credit reports.

This is a great way to start your children's credit education, too.

The overnight addition to a credit's age, limit, and payment history can boost a score hundreds of points.

AU accounts are so effective for boosting credit scores that many unscrupulous credit services actually sell them as "Seasoned Trade lines".

First of all, buying a trade line for the purpose of qualifying for financing, like a home mortgage, is fraud. You could go to jail or receive a hefty fine.

Second, FICO knows about Seasoned Trade lines and has made adjustments. When those adjustments hit the scoring model lenders use, then those trade lines will become worthless.

Third, you don't need to buy trade lines anyway. Simply ask a family member, or someone you've shared an address with, to add you as an AU.

Tell them you don't need or want a card, but you want your credit score to benefit from their good credit history.

Look for a card from a major lender with a high limit, low balance, and perfect payment history. The older the card the better.

Refinance Revolving Debt

Any time you pay off your credit cards your score is going to go up.

Refinancing your revolving debt with an instalment loan is a way to game the system into thinking you have less debt.

FICO doesn't give as much weight to instalment loans, so adding the equivalent instalment debt while paying off revolving debt will have an overall positive effect on your score.

Just don't go running up your cards while you're paying off your instalment loan or you'll end up with twice the debt.

That's a recipe for disaster.

Day 16 - Refinance Revolving Debt with a Home Equity Loan

Using a Home Equity Loan (HEL) to pay off your revolving debts will improve your credit scores for the same reason using any other instalment loan to pay off your revolving debt would work.

FICO gives less weight to instalment loan debt.

You just need to make sure you use a Home Equity LOAN and not a Home Equity Line of Credit (HELOC).

A HELOC is scored just like a credit card by FICO, so using it wouldn't improve your scores.

Just be sure to use it to pay down your debt and not as a way to get yourself into more debt.

If you're not disciplined enough to not run up your balances again, then this would not be a smart move for you.

I include it because it works, but you have to pick and choose what works for YOU.

Credit Builder Loans

Some lenders offer a secured loan program designed to help you rebuild your credit.

They're called Credit Builder Loans.

This is a very effective, all be it slow, method for boosting your scores. It's slower because it's an instalment loan. Installment loans have less of an impact on your credit score.

Be that as it may, over 6-12 months you will see a credit score increase. That's because you need a few instalment loans to improve the "Credit Mix" which is responsible for 10% of your credit score.

Here's how your scores are determined:

FICO SCORES IMAGE

Ideal ratio is:

2-4 credit cards

A car loan, home loan, and personal loan

1-2 retail cards

The credit builder loan completes the personal loan portion of the equation.

Here's how it work;

The amount you borrow is deposited into an escrow account. You can't touch it until the loan is paid. You make your regular payments each month, building your credit score as you go. When you're done paying, you get the full balance plus interest, to do with as you please.

Traditional features include:

Loan amounts from $500-$3000

12-24 month terms

Loan funds earn dividends

Loan interest rate is fixed at 5%

So, for example, a $1000 loan at 5% over 18 months would equal payments of $57.79.

The terms may change from bank to bank so you need to shop around.

Credit Scoring Models

These are specialized agencies that develop scoring formats for credit bureaus. According to the Federal Statistics, there are over 50 of them in the United States. Of that, only FICO, a model designed by Fair

Isaac Company, is widely used and accepted everywhere. It is often adopted by the three most popular credit bureaus in the country too. Fairly, FICO is trailed by Vantage, Community Empower, Trans union, Xpert, Insurance, and some others.

Due to this diversity, it is impossible to generate an all-purpose method of calculating credit scores. So, it would be impossible to tell how each company measures your credit performance concisely. It is clear however, these scoring models usually generate 3-digit as your credit score, which means you may rank anywhere between 300- 850 (or 950).

Chapter 2. The Importance of a Good Credit Score

A good relationship is significant for enhancing the creditworthiness of the market. It can help you in many ways and talk about your clean background. It reflects your personality and your character. Employers also prefer someone with a good score and a clean relationship. It is synonymous with sensitivity and responsibility. If you're at a loss and don't know how to improve your score, check out our credit guide.

How to Get Help?

At this point, as you read this article, you may experience the following problems.

- A poor or falling credit rating.
- Think about foreclosure or filing for bankruptcy.
- Invoices or credit card loans over the limit or pending.

- Threats for non-payment of bills, loans or mortgages.

Faced with one of these problems, you can get help from a variety of sources. These financial difficulties are common and can force you to lose your way. Several companies and agents are waiting to attract such gullible customers. They can mislead you and cause you further difficulties. You could work in your interest instead of in your interest. Several agencies of this type have unsatisfied customers who have been deceived. If you want to resolve your situation and work on the current financial situation, you need to read the relevant guide. Here are some ways you can improve your scores.

Tips to Improve Your Score

Plastic Money - The first thing you need to do to improve your score is to stop using plastic money. If you've already created a large invoice, you can order it, but no longer use the card. Reduce your purchases for a while until you are in control of the situation again.

Report - Request a report and rate the area you need to work on. You also need to carefully review the reports to determine if there are errors. Check for incorrect information. Has it corrected by writing to the office about it?

Pay your bills on time - use your salary to pay your bills on time. Don't be late in paying. Late payment not only involves fees and expenses but is also reflected negatively in the relationship.

Don't fall victim to scam repair - discover the federal law that governs this system. Some people fall victim to such repair agencies. It is better to face the situation alone. If necessary, contact the State Commission for more information on the procedure. You can also read books on credit. It's important to keep the situation under control before it gets worse and makes you fail.

Importance of a Good Credit Score?

The credit score is a numerical expression for the statistical analysis of credit files. In simple terms, this number will help you prove your creditworthiness. The score measures past ability to repay loans and manage previously granted loans. It is usually based on the reporting information of the credit bureau. You will rely on wounds to reduce losses when it comes to bad debt. It is the outcomes that can determine who is eligible for a loan and which interest rates are most appropriate, including the credit limits that individuals receive.

Credit scores can also say a lot about your character and personality and linger forever. You will never benefit from poor results in financial situations that must occur throughout your life. You can also use numbers to evaluate employers, which makes having a good score very important. It will represent your level of responsibility and sensitivity.

When buying a home: a home is a huge investment that can be very difficult to make. A home loan may be needed to make your dreams come true.

When buying a car: vehicle loans are among the most popular. Auto loans don't seem to be home loans. It is, therefore, possible to get along with bad credit scores. However, if you have bad credit, you will end up paying very high yield loans with your auto loan. The deposit is also higher for you if you have a band score.

When starting a business: Just like buying a house or car, financial support may be needed to start a business. The credit rating depends on your eligibility for that loan. This can seriously affect your ability to access a corporate loan when it is needed.

Looking for work: Nowadays, employers also run credit checks when they want to hire new employees. It is especially common in the financial sector and government institutions. A negative score can be an obstacle to this job, so it is important to maintain good credit scores.

You will also find it very important to check your credit report. A thorough review helps to identify errors. You will likewise get numerous tips and guidance on the best way to improve your credit ratings to keep up a cleaner register before you need money or business help. There are excellent websites out there that will help you check and calculate your scores and even get a free copy of them.

Before doing any real estate business, you need to know a few things about your balance. First, a copy of all three credit reports (Trans Union, Equifax and Experian) is required, which can be easily found online in this era of computer information.

The primary concern you need to search for in your momentum reports is the point at which you have recorded antagonistic data. "Unwanted information" includes things like late payments, collections, judgments, etc. If you have negative information about your relationships and have the money to pay for them, do it immediately. The better your credit, the more business you can do. However, as mentioned above, you can do business if you have bad credit. It's easier if you don't.

The accompanying table will enable you to comprehend where your credit is found:

Credit score / rating

700 or more / excellent (A + credit)

This score indicates that in the past three years, there have been no significant delays (60 days or more) for any type of loan payment. These people can get slightly better interest rates on some types of loans.

699-660 / Very good (credit)

659-620 / Voucher (one credit)

These values do not result in significant payments (60 days or more) overdue for a mortgage loan in the past two years and only a few small delays in loan payments over the past two years. These people can quickly get "market interest rates" on all types of loans, including public loans. Bankruptcies must be resolved and resolved for four years to be classified as "good".

619-590 / Fair (credit B)

This score indicates some significant delays (60 or more days) for a mortgage loan in the past two years and widespread minor delays in loan payments over the past three years. These people receive slightly higher interest rates for all types of loans, except for public loans (FHA, VA), which are not based solely on credit scores.

589-480 / Bad (credit C)

This score indicates MANY significant delays (60 days or more) overdue for a mortgage in the past two years and widespread MAJOR payments (60-90 days) for loan payments over the past three years. People with a C loan generally receive higher interest rates and higher equity or a higher down payment for all types of loans except public loans.

In most cases, 520 is the type of approval limit for portfolio loan buyers whose loans are led by actions. Bankruptcies must be paid at the time of applying for a loan to be classified as "bad". Current amortizations, bad debts and sentences sometimes don't have to be repaid to get a mortgage. However, the penalty is a small pool of lenders, high-interest rates and stiff prepayment penalties if you refinance within three years.

Another factor in deciding your financial assessment is the number of solicitations you have. Numerous applications are dismissed because the candidate has an excessive amount of solicitations. As a general rule, "too many" requests are defined as more than 6-8 requests in your credit report. Credit bureaus have informed creditors that a person with more than this in their credit report is jumping around looking for credit, generally indicating that they are desperate or inattentive. Of course, they never think that you could simply look for the best loan.

If you have more than 6-8 requests in your credit reports, the new FCRA (Fair Credit Reporting Act) states that no requests can remain in your report for more than a year. If your report shows previous requests, you can remove duplicate requests.

It is essential to know your balance. If your score is between 620 and 700 or more, you can negotiate better conditions and interest rates on your loans. But if your credit is lower, you can still get credit, but all you have to do is "turn" and take a higher interest rate until your credit improves.

Before doing business, we cannot stress the importance of knowing your balance.

1. A borrower with a score of 680+ is considered for an A + loan. This type of loan includes the essential subscription, probably through a "computerized automated subscription" system, which is completed in a few minutes and can be completed in a few days.

2. A borrower with a score below 680 but over 620 will find that lenders take a closer look when applying for a loan. Additional credit documents and explanations may be requested before making a subscription decision.

3. A borrower with a score below 620 can be excluded from the best loan rates and conditions. These borrowers are usually redirected to alternative funding sources.

Remember, just because your credit isn't A +, with patience and some creative funding, you can still do the business you want to do. Your credit can and will consistently change, and as you begin working together and reimbursing these loan specialists, it will bit by bit increment. This makes financing your offers simpler and more straightforward. Be quiet and constant and recall the significance of knowing your equalization.

You need to know what's in your credit report before you can find out what you need to do to improve it.

Check the credit report

The single score provides a snapshot of your credit status and is determined by a series of factors that can be divided into... like what will happen to credit history - how long have you been using credit.

Payment history

Do you have a history of paying bills on time...

25

Chapter 3.   How to Boost Your Credit Score

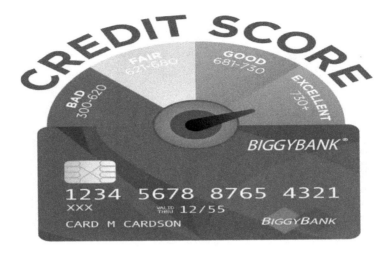

You need to know what is in your credit report before you can find out what you need to do to change it.

Check the credit report

The credit score provides a snapshot of your credit status and is determined by a series of factors that can be divided into the following categories: credit history - How long have you been using credit?

Payment History

Do you have a history of paying on time?

Credit amount - How much do you do and how much do you owe?

Check over your credit report with a fine-tooth comb: verify that the amount due for each account is accurate. And look for all the accounts you paid off that still show as outstanding issues. Pay particular attention to any requests for recent information that you have not authorized. Before an endorsing creditor, or someone pretending to be you, for an account, they will make a request that will be indicated on your credit report.

Checking your credit report on a regular basis, at least once a year, is a good way to collect any cases where you could be the target of identity theft - or the credit bureau has accidentally mixed your story with someone similar name.

Pay early and often (or at least, on time)

Credit reports record payment habits on all types of bills and extended credit, not just credit cards. And sometimes these objects show up on their own official report, but not that of another. Old, unpaid gymnastic odds that only appear on a relationship could be affecting your score without even realizing it.

A full one-third of your score depends on whether you pay your creditors on time. So, make sure you pay all your bills by their due dates, including rent/mortgage, utilities, doctor's bills, etc. Keep documentation (such as checks or cancelled receipts) to be able to prove that you have done the punctuality of payments.

The Fair Isaac Corporation, which calculates FICO scores, recommends signing up for payment notices if the lender makes them available. Another approach is to create automatic drafts from your bank account.

Pick up a payment order

When using your cards, try to pay them off as soon as you can (you do not need to wait for the instruction in the mail, but you can pay online at any time).

Do not open too many accounts

If you shop at that store, it can often be worth getting your card; otherwise, resist the temptation. What is more, every time you apply for credit the potential lender will check your score. Whenever the credit is selected, other potential lenders worry about the additional debt that they can take on. Sometimes, the act of opening a new account, or even applying for one, can lower the score; have a lot of recent inquiries about your credit report dings your score temporarily. So do not ask for the card often if you want to increase your credit score.

Do not close credit cards

A good idea would be to keep three or four credit card accounts open but use only one or two of them; put away or cut the others. Once you have paid a card, however, keep the account open, even if you do not want to use it anymore. In closing, late accounts or those with a history of late payments can also help, as long as you have paid them in full. Because history is important if you decide to close a couple of accounts, close the most recent ones. Be sure to use these cards to make occasional purchases (so pay the bills in full), so the card company does not close the account due to inactivity.

Increase the credit limit

There is a way to increase your credit score that does not involve paying a debt or any of the other more traditional credit score tactics by increasing. Since credit scores are determined, in part, on the difference between the credit limit and the amount of credit used, ask for a higher credit limit. Your chances of increasing it are probably better than you think. Of those applying for a higher credit limit, 8 out of 10 have been approved, according to a recent money survey. While it helps to be over 30, there is a good chance for all adults. To prevent the credit decreased with the request for a higher limit, to ask for the highest credit line increase that does not trigger what is called a difficult request.

By increasing the credit limit, the differential between the amount you are allowed to borrow and the amount you actually make is automatically increased. The larger the spread, the higher the credit score.

The credit utilization report

This spread, known as the credit utilization ratio, is expressed as a percentage. For example, if the limit on the MasterCard is $ 5,000 and you have a budget of $ 4,000, the usage ratio is 80%. If you request a credit line increase and the limit goes up to $ 10,000, suddenly your use is only 40%.

Obviously, the higher the percentage, the worse you look. Experts have long said that using 30% of available credit is a good way to keep your credit score high. More recently, this recommendation has been reduced to 20%. In the $ 5000 MasterCard limit example above, 30% usage would represent a

$ 1,500 balance. Increasing the credit limit from $ 5,000 to $ 10,000 would allow a $ 3,000 balance and still maintain 30% utilization. This is also the reason why you should not close your accounts, which will increase the percentage of total available credit that you are using - and which will reduce your score.

Negotiate a lower interest rate

However, the key to this strategy is getting more credit, but no longer using credit. In other words, if the limit goes up to $ 1,000, do not go out and half responsible for it. Think of the push as a way to save money when applying for a car loan, home loan or another form of long-term debt where a high credit score will probably lead to big savings through a rate of lower interest.

Chapter 4. Credit Scoring Myth

For a large portion of credit scoring's history, by far, most of the people engaged with loaning decisions pretty much needed to think about what hurt or helped a score. Makers of scoring formulas would not like to uncover much about how the models functioned, for dread that contenders would take their thoughts or that consumers would make sense of how to beat the framework. Luckily, today we discover much increasingly about credit scoring—however, not every person has stayed aware of the latest knowledge. Mortgage intermediaries, loan officials, credit agency agents, credit guides, and the media, among others, continue to spread outdated and out and out bogus information. Following up on their terrible guidance can put your score and your accounts at critical risk.

Here are probably the most widely recognized fantasies.

Myth 1: Closing Credit Accounts Will Help Your Score

This one sounds sensible, particularly when a mortgage merchant discloses to you that lenders are suspicious of people who have heaps of unused credit accessible to them. All what's you, all things considered, from hurrying out and charging up a tempest? Obviously, looking at the situation objectively, what's shielded you from piling on huge balances before now? If you've been responsible with credit before, you're probably going to continue to be responsible later. That is the essential standard behind credit scoring: Its rewards practices that show moderate, responsible utilization of credit after some time, because those propensities are probably going to continue.

The score likewise rebuffs conduct that is not all that responsible, for example, applying for a lot of credit you don't require. Numerous people with high credit scores locates that one of only a handful hardly any detriments for them is the number of credit accounts recorded on their reports. At the point when they go to get their credit scores, they're informed that one reason their score isn't considerably higher is that they have "too many open accounts." Many mistakenly expect they can "fix" this issue by closing accounts. In any case, after you've opened the accounts, you've done the damage. You can't fix it by closing the account. You can, however, make matters more awful.

Myth 2: You Can Increase Your Score by Asking Your Credit Card Company to Lower Your Limits

This one is a minor departure from the possibility that decreasing your accessible credit by one way or another enables your score by making you to appear to be less risky to lenders. By and by, it's missing the goal. Narrowing the difference between the credit you use and the credit you have accessible to you can negatively affect your score. It doesn't make a difference that you requested the decrease; the FICO formula doesn't recognize lower limits that you mentioned and lower limits forced by a creditor. All it sees is less difference between your balances and your limits, and that is not good. If that, you need to enable your score, to handle the issue from the opposite end: by paying down your debt. Expanding the gap between your balance and your credit limit positively affects your score.

Myth 3: You Need to Pay Interest to Obtain a Good Credit Score

This is the precise inverse of the past myth, and it's similarly as misinformed. It is not necessary for you to carry a balance on your credit cards and pay interest to have a good score. As you've perused a few times as of now, your credit reports—and subsequently the FICO formula—make no differentiation between balances you carry month to month and balances that you pay off. Savvy consumers don't carry credit card balances under any circumstances, and not to improve their scores. Presently, the facts confirm that to get the highest FICO scores, you must have both revolving accounts, for example, credit cards, and instalment loans, for example, a mortgage or car loan. What's more, except for those 0 per cent rates used to drive auto deals after Sept. 11, most instalment loans require paying interest.

Yet, here's a news streak: You don't have to have the highest score to get good credit. Any score more than 720 or so will get you the best rates and terms with numerous lenders. A few, particularly auto and home value lenders, save their best bargains for those with scores more than 760. You don't must have an 850, or even 800 score, to get incredible arrangements. In case you're attempting to improve a fair score, a little, reasonable instalment loan can help—if you can get affirmed for it and pay it off on time. However, some way or another, there's no motivation to stray into the red and pay interest.

Myth 4: Your Closed Accounts Should Indicate "Closed by Consumer," Or They Will Hurt Your Score

The hypothesis behind this myth is that lenders will see a closed account on your credit report and, if not educated generally, will accept that a nauseated creditor cut you off because you botched in some way or another. Obviously, as you most likely are aware at this point, numerous lenders never observe your real report. They're simply taking a gander at your credit score, which couldn't care less who closed a credit card. Fair Isaac figures that if a lender closes your account, it's either for dormancy or because you defaulted. If that you defaulted, that will be sufficiently archived in the account's history. If it makes you feel better to contact the bureaus and guarantee that accounts you closed are recorded as "closed by consumer," by all methods do as such. However, it won't make any distinction to your credit score.

Myth 5: Credit Counselling Is Way Worse Than Bankruptcy

Sometimes this is expressed as "credit advising is as awful as bankruptcy" or "credit directing is as terrible as bankruptcy." None of these statements is valid. A bankruptcy recording is the single most noticeably terrible thing you can do to your credit score. On the other hand, the current FICO formula totally ignores any reference to credit guiding that may be on your credit report. Credit guiding is treated as an impartial factor, neither aiding nor hurting your score. Credit guides, if you're inexperienced with the term, have practical experience in arranging lower interest rates and also working out payment plans for debtors that may some way or another file for bankruptcy. Although credit advisors may consolidate the consumer's bills into one monthly payment, they don't give loans—as debt consolidators do—or guarantee to wipe out or settle debts for not exactly the chief amount you owe.

The fact that credit guiding itself won't affect your score doesn't mean, notwithstanding, that enrolling in a credit advisor's debt management plan will leave your credit sound. A few lenders will report you as late only for enrolling in a debt management plan. Their thinking is that you're not paying them what you initially owed, so you ought to need to endure some agony. That is not, by any means, the only way you could be reported late. Not all credit instructors are made equivalent, and some have been blamed for retaining consumer payments that were proposed for creditors.

Chapter 5.   How Credit System Works

In a nutshell, the entire credit system constitutes the credit bureaus, the creditors and you. Creditors are the companies you access credit from while the credit bureaus collect credit data from past and current creditors and compile it into reports, which are modelled in the form of credit profiles for each credit consumer, after which they sell these reports to creditors so that they can make various decisions.

The creditors use the data they obtain from credit bureaus to determine how much they will charge you for borrowing and the amount of penalties they should charge you for defaulting. Whenever a creditor needs credit profiles of people that have a certain credit score, they buy that information from the credit bureaus. This helps them to target their products and services since they will then send emails to those in that list enticing them to buy or use their products and services. It is believed that most of these companies go after those that have a low score. This will allow them to have a chance at making a greater profit and pulling out as much money as possible from these people's pockets.

The credit system consists of three parties namely you, the creditors, and the credit bureaus.

If a creditor needs a report of credit consumers who have a specific credit score, they can then buy the credit profiles from the credit bureaus thus making it easy to target products and services appropriately. They (creditors) will send you enticing information on offers that you should buy.

Subprime credit data is the best-selling for the different credit reporting agencies. Therefore, if you have a subprime credit rating. You are likely to be getting countless email solicitations for you to apply to different credit cards. The reasoning for this is straight forward. With a subprime credit rating, you are going to be charged more for accessing credit. This simply means that the lenders will make more money from you. If you have excellent credit rating, you are low risk and lenders charge you less for accessing credit, which means that they make less money when they advance your credit. In other terms, lenders will want to prey on you if you have bad credit because they are certain that they will make more money in the end. Even if you are to default, you are likely to have paid more money than someone who has good credit! Subprime data is such a hot selling product that the credit reporting agencies charge more for it; it is in high demand! This can be translated to mean that the creditors and credit bureaus don't care about you having good credit. In any case, if your credit rating is bad, they will charge you more! Do you know that over 90 per cent of credit reports have been proven to have inaccurate, unverifiable, and erroneous entries?

Well, now you know why your credit score is always becoming bad even with all your effort. These companies are in it for profit. They will even overlook when erroneous entries are posted in your report. In any case, they have convinced us to think that the reports are the gospel truth when they are nowhere close to that. So, in simple terms, these 2 players in the credit system can only be compelled by the law to put things in order. They have no interest in you having perfect credit because they all make more money if you have bad credit.

If you are in this group of credit consumers, you will get the most enticing offers and email solicitations to apply for credit cards. The reason is simple, as was mentioned, when your credit score isn't so good, the creditors will charge more for advancing your credit, which means that they make more money. In financial terms, creditors address their exposure to credit risk through charging more for credit. If you have the capacity to pay the right amount on time this will cause them to lose out on a substantial amount of profit. They will not be satisfied with what they receive and will want more out of their customers. They might not directly refuse you credit but will not be particularly interested in giving you money. They will be waiting for someone with bad credit to walk in. When you have poor credit, you might be paying up to three times what you would pay were you to have a perfect credit score.

So, the companies will expressly go after those that have a bad score and will put in all possible effort to trap them. As you can see, creditors will be inclined to prey on those with sub-prime credit score for the simple reason that they will make more money from them even if they were to default as they will have made money already! So, there is a lot of planning that they do just to fill up their pockets.

It should not surprise you that these companies work hand in hand. It takes effort from both ends for their schemes to work and they will ensure that they are on the same page. They will come up with plans that will benefit both and cause each to make a large profit at the expense of the customer. Imagine trying to cheat millions of customers on a yearly basis, it is a Herculean task and will require the company to be as prepared as possible to pull it off with ease. For this reason, they will join hands and make sure each one cuts into the profit.

Apart from these 2, there will be some third parties who will work to help these credit companies. These can be outsourced companies or independent ones looking to hook up with the credit companies and trying to make money for themselves. These will have the exclusive job of looking for people that have not checked their records for some time and determine to get them on board. They will put in a lot of effort to catch these people's fancy and once they trap them, they will direct them to the credit company and get them to pay for their services.

To prove that your bad credit history records are a best seller for credit reporting agencies, do you know that they will even charge more to credit providers to access such information. That's right, they will pay up a little extra just to find those that have a bad credit and start bombarding them with emails that ask them to apply for credit at their place. This means that none of these parties has any specific interest to have the information in your credit report reported accurately.

Do you know that only a small percentage of people file disputes for such items despite over 90 per cent of credit reports having been found to have erroneous, unverifiable and inaccurate entries? Many will not wish to go through the pain of proving themselves right. This allows the companies to have a long leash and they will not back away from exploiting these people. The companies have several good field days owing to such ignorance on the part of the customers.

The credit companies will be determined to report your bad credit and this means that some of them will even let such entries be included in your credit report for the simple reason that so few of us have the guts to challenge entries in the credit report even if they are incorrect, unverifiable and erroneous. They will know who exactly will not challenge it just by looking at your credit history. They will not have an interest in catering to those that might take up a dispute. They will employ people to especially look for those customers that have a bad score and those that look most likely to remain mum about errors in their reports.

The 2 other players in the credit system (the creditors and the credit reporting agencies) are in it to make the most money from you directly or indirectly so counting on them to help you make things right should be out of the question. The more screwed up your credit score is, the more money there is to be made by the credit reporting agencies and the creditors. That is, the lower the score, the better their prospects to charge you a bomb.

So, when you file a dispute, the creditors and the credit reporting agencies will only update the data - not because they have any interest in your welfare - but because they don't have an option given to them and they are under legal obligation to act in accordance with the law. They will not expressly pursue your cause and, in fact, despite your efforts to fix your bad score, they will try and remain ignorant of it and make things worse for you. They will go to any lengths just to make sure that you have no chance of fixing your score despite none of it being your fault.

This is the exact reason why there are hundreds, probably thousands, of people who despise credit card companies. They will not stop at anything and fall to the absolute lows just to make a few extra dollars. Many of these companies will have a bad reputation and yet find easy prey for themselves. They will know how exactly they can target the customers and get them to subscribe to their card. Once the person is trapped, they will not stop until they fulfil their desire to make as much money as possible. The poor customer will be trapped and will have to surrender to the demands of the vicious company.

Every day, there are hundreds of innocent customers who fall for this trick and do not put in the effort to check their credit reports. But it is important for every person to thoroughly go through their report and look for any erroneous and wrong entries that may be causing them their low scores.

Now that you understand that only yourself is on your side on matters pertaining the accuracy of the credit report, how do you know how your credit score affects your ability to borrow? It is apparent that your score is the most vital element in your report and something that needs to be investigated carefully. But what is this score and what are its parameters? How do you know that your score is good, average or bad?

Of course the report doesn't state that a certain amount is bad, so understanding what benchmarks the lenders are going to use in categorizing you as good (perfect), average (sub-prime) and bad will be very helpful so that you know what to expect when you see that number on your credit report.

Chapter 6.   Protect Your Credit: Credit Monitoring

It means monitoring and inspecting your credit history as shown on your credit report. In the end, that is really what it is all about, your credit report and more importantly unexpected changes to your credit report. A credit monitoring service provides this monitoring service for you (for a fee, of course). Most credit monitoring services report that they monitor and track your credit report daily.

What Happens with Credit Monitoring?

When you sign up with a credit monitoring company, they pull all your information from all three credit reporting agencies and typically ask if you are in the process of applying for new credit. Often, they will ask you to check the credit report and verify the information. Of course, they will want to know about any activity you consider suspicious. Now, your new credit monitoring service has a baseline or starting point. Any changes to your credit report going forward could be flagged as possibly fraudulent. Depending on the options available and the monitoring plan you chose, you will be alerted to any suspicious activity that could affect your credit report.

The credit monitoring companies typically are on the alert for:

- New credit inquiries

- Delinquencies

- Negative information that suddenly shows up

- Employment changes

- New credit accounts

- Increased credit lines at existing accounts

- Other changes to your credit report that could be considered a red flag for identity theft

You should note that one reason credit monitoring services have become so popular lately is their alerts for suspicious activity on your credit report is viewed as a counter to identity theft. Some credit monitoring companies even promote their services with this claim.

Advantages

- Constant Tracking - All of your credit reports are constantly tracked. Depending on your choice of credit monitoring companies and plans, this monitoring could be daily or weekly.

- Increased Knowledge - about your own credit. During the time you use a credit monitoring service, you will gain an incredibly valuable firsthand knowledge of how personal credit actually works. Simply by watching the reports provided from your credit monitoring service, you will see in real time how your credit report changes. You will see how even small actions on your part can have a sizeable effect on your credit score. For example, you can watch your credit score drop right after you applied for four different department store credit cards.

- It does not Cost, it saves - Yes, this is a tired old cliché, yet here it truly works. Consider it this way: suppose you use your new knowledge of how your personal credit works, how small things affect your credit score, and that sort of thing to get a better loan rate. Really, it is that easy. For example, let us say you use your newfound credit wisdom to raise your credit score by 75 points.

- Identity Theft Protection - Since your credit report is under constant scrutiny, detection of possible fraudulent activity happens much faster. The credit monitoring service helps you both detect and minimize damage from malicious use of your personal financial information. Additionally, many credit monitoring companies offer legal protections and financial reimbursements. These reimbursements can range from $25,000 to $1,000,000. Surely you have seen the advertisements with the big-name credit monitoring service offering their one-million-dollar guarantee.

- Faster Resolution of Errors - Should you spot an error on one of your many reports sent to you by your credit monitoring service, most of them will assist you in correcting the error.

- No More Guesswork - Since you are paying for professional credit monitoring. Additionally, since your credit monitoring service will alert you for any suspicious activities, you are always aware of what is happening with your credit.

- Less Hassle for You - Yes, credit monitoring can be done yourself as will be explained shortly. However, paying for a credit monitoring service eliminates one more thing for you to do.

Disadvantages

- Price - Of course, all of the services provided by credit monitoring companies comes at a price. Price is one common complaint against credit monitoring companies. Each company sets their own pricing structure. Also, many of them offer different levels of service at different price points.

- Information Disparity - The information available from one credit monitoring service can be vastly different from another credit monitoring service.

- Cancellation Issues - There are various reports (complaints) from past customers of some credit monitoring services regarding the difficulty encountered in cancelling the service.

- Micromanagement Time Wastes - Because your new credit monitoring service provides you with frequent reports and analysis, you may end up trying to micromanage your credit score. This micromanagement could end up costing you a lot of time with few if any substantive changes to your credit score.

- False Sense of Security - Since you are paying for a credit monitoring service, the tendency is to fall into the trap of that is all you need to do to protect yourself. Identity theft protection involves additional areas beyond your credit report that you still need to monitor.

- A Credit Monitoring Service cannot do it as fast as You Might Want - It is not yet possible to monitor a person's credit history on a real time basis. For one thing, many creditors only report information on existing clients weekly or even monthly.

- A Credit Monitoring Service is not the Final Solution - Even the very best credit monitoring service is not capable of fully identifying all fraudulent activity. Consider that there are many credit details that are never even reported to a credit reporting agency.

Chapter 7.   Controlling Various Kinds of Debt

Common Types of Debts

It depends on how you choose to see this. There are different kinds or types of debts. We will cut them into four groups to make this fun. Now, the first group.

1. Secured and Unsecured Loans.

Secured loans

Secured loans are the types of debts you get by offering something as surety in case you don't pay that money up. As an example, if you are buying a house, a car, or getting a big work machine, you may opt for a loan when you don't have enough funds to clear the bills yourself. Often, that is a lot of money, and your credit company wants to be sure you're paying it all without complications. So, you are asked to mortgage some of your valued assets in turn. They keep the documents until your payment is complete. If you don't pay up, there are a few legal actions to make, and they sell the assets. The norm is that you take this type of loan on significant assets.

Unsecured loans

Unsecured loans are the direct opposite of secured loans. You do not have to stake anything to access a loan like this. All you need is indicate your interest, submit your essential documents, and the loan is yours. The type of loan you're asking for is what determines what you will be submitting. For example, your credit report may just be enough to get you another credit card. You may have to drop a little deposit plus your credit report when you're signing up for some utilities. All of these have a little or minimal risk by the user. Only that you can cover simple services with this type of loan, no more. Now, you can imagine which weighs higher on a credit score ranked by FICO.

2. Fixed and Revolving Payment Method

Fixed Payment Method

A lot of times, your credit company lays out clear terms, duration, and method of payment to you.

When this happens, we say you have got a fixed payment method. Usually, fixed payment methods attract fixed interests too. When you take part in a dealership deal, for example, you may be graced to get that money paid at a particular amount each month and a particular interest rate. Say, the car is worth a thousand USD. You are allowed to pay up in two years, with a total interest of 30%. That is pretty straightforward, right? That's just how fixed payment loans work. A mortgage is an example of fixed payment loans, so you might say they are pretty standard.

Revolving Payment Method:

These types of loans are those that swing like unpredictable bells. There are no exact modalities on most items. You simply take the loans and pay as you can. For example, you can pay when you have the funds; there is no exact deadline for payments. You don't get a limit to interest rates too. Often, your utility, as well as your credit card, fall into this category. This is the exact reason you draw up a credit card, and you can use the credit card as much as you like each month. You don't have to pay up that money when the month ends. You can pay a little now, a lot more over the coming months. But as FICO had earlier advised, it makes perfect sense to draw up only 30% or less of your credit limits. Expectedly, your interest rate is determined by how promptly you clear off that debt.

3. Good and Bad Loans

No questions, this list can't be closed if this group isn't here.

The Good Loans

Classifying loans as good or bad does not exist in official records. Maybe if it did, nobody would ever be excited to try out the bad ones. In any case, a good loan is any loan drawn to invest in resources that may become useful and available over a long period, sometimes, forever. Some of them are:

Mortgage: If it is damning to size up your mortgage and you are planning to hand over the building, my sincere suggestion is that you keep pulling through, and you remain upbeat. This is one of the loans you can't ever regret taking. It is glaring to anyone that houses are assets that you don't use up any moment soon. A house may get into a bad shape sometimes. That's normal. You are expected to keep it brimming with brightness naturally. If you do things right, you can't ever have to pay rents. You also have an asset you can risk to get huge loans to build your career. If things get worse, you can auction the house and restart your careers somewhere. However, you choose to see it, a loan drawn to get a house is a good one. Just be sure you can keep paying till the end before drawing the loan at all.

Student Loans: Well, you might hear someone say drawing student loan in insane. But if you look over the sayings, you'd have something different. You've got to get a good education, and you can't afford it at that moment. It makes perfect sense to tangle yourself in a loan, bag that degree, and pay back much more quickly. As you may fear, your first few years after school would be spent clearing your old debt. But you become free soon, and you'd have access to opportunities you may not have found without top training. From all viewpoints you see this, it is a win-win for all teams. So, I'd vote this as a good loan!

Business: Now, this is another perspective. If you are getting the loans to jack up your investments, you are settling for a good one too. It is undoubtedly a risk, since the business may pick up and may not. But if you probably play your cards right, your business can boom, and that is the start of a goal you didn't see coming.

So, Bad Loans?

Auto loans: For a fact, you must be curious to know why auto loans should be tagged a bad debt, isn't it? I bet! Well, it is. Auto Loans, dealerships, and whatever kind of car loan you get into is a bad loan. This is because cars are not assets that can be used for a long while. If you sign a two or five-year loan deal, your car is already developing some sorts of problems. So, you'd have to spend on it, and at that same time, pay your auto loans. It would be a mess in a few years.

Credit Card Loans: Credit Card Loans are probably the worst you can take. They can't be used to get important stuff. And either you take note or not, your debt is on the rise with every month you forgot to clear up.

Most Other loans: Most of the other types of loans fall into this category, especially those you draw from friends and family. They are often not precisely significant and should be avoided. Except, of course, they are critical to you, and you are sure there's some way you can quickly pay it all back.

How to Control Your Credit

Regardless of what credit types you have drawn, it is vital to monitor and control it all before it gets out of hand. Even if it's slipped a bit, the best option you've got is to find some way to monitor and control it. Hence, I'll be showing you some easy and practical ways in the next few lines. Here;

1. Don't let things slip off: That's the first rule. Prevention is way better than cure. It stands to reason that if you can plan

appropriately and watch out for sinking moments, you shouldn't have to fight to save your credit score fiercely. All you need is to do the math. Where are you heading to? What are your chances of hitting it big or terribly crashing? What would you have to do to avoid falling into a debt pit and struggling to pay up? Several things we might say. Your first job is to find those targets and set them working.

2. Don't spend payments: Pending payments only increase your penalties. Whether for fixed and revolving debts. So, with the facts that you should avoid pending your payments. Clear them off the instant you are able to.

3. Don't toy with revolving debts: Revolving debts are full of surprises. You would usually assume they are the littlest, and so, they can be paid after the much bigger debts. In reality, your revolving debts (like your credit cards) cart away more than your

fixed debts. They tend to increase all the time, and there's a high potential for interest increase too, which doesn't happen in fixed credit cases. Hence, it washes that you should pay them up before considering some other debts at all. Don't delay others too!

If you do the math and your revolving debts are out, you will have a concrete idea of how to tackle the only other debts you have left. This itself is an acute style of controlling debts that you didn't notice. Now you know, cheers.

Chapter 8.   Fixing Your Credit Score Fast

Credit bureaus have 30 days to examine complaints and frequently concede to what lenders state about you, regardless of whether it's valid. Regardless of whether all parties concur that a mistake has been made, the errors can continue to manifest in your file on account of the automated idea of most credit reporting. You may need to contact creditors and the bureaus a few times to get mistakes erased. The process may take weeks; best case scenario, you may be taking on the conflict for quite a long time or even years. In case you're amidst attempting to get a mortgage, these errors can cause significant problems. You probably won't have sufficient opportunity to fix your report before the house drops out of escrow or you stall out with an interest rate a lot higher than you have the right to pay.

Issues, for example, these might entice you to turn to one of the numerous organizations that guarantee "moment credit fix" or that assurance to help your credit score. No authentic organization makes such guarantees or certifications, however, so any individual who employs one of these outfits is asking to be misled. There are, in any case, a developing number of certified administrations that can actually fix your credit report errors in 72 hours or less. Read on to learn more.

Fixing Your Credit in a Matter of Hours: Rapid Rescoring

Rapid rescoring administrations came about in light of the fact that such a large number of people were losing loans or paying an excess of interest on account of credit bureau mistakes. Before you get energized, however, you ought to learn what these administrations can and can't do:

- They can't manage you straightforwardly as a consumer—Rapid rescoring is typically offered by little credit-reporting agencies, which fill in as a kind of go between the bureaus and the lending experts. These agencies, which are frequently free, however, which may be auxiliaries of credit bureaus, provide uncommon administrations for loan officials and mortgage representatives, for example, blended or "3-in-1" credit reports. To profit by rapid rescoring, you should work with a loan official or mortgage representative who buys in to an agency that offers the administration.

- They can help you just in the event that you have proof, or if proof can be obtained—Rapid rescoring administrations aren't intended to help people who presently can't seem to begin the credit-fix process. You need something in writing, for example, a letter from the creditor recognizing that your account was reported as late when you were actually reality on time. (This is one reason that it's so necessary to get everything in writing when you're attempting to fix your credit.) If you don't have such proof, however, the creditor has recognized the error, some rapid recorders can get the proof for you. Nonetheless, that may add days or weeks to the process.

- They can assist you with getting errors fixed; however, they can't remove genuine negative things that are in dispute—also, you need proof that a mistake was made—not simply your say as much. If that the credit bureau is already researching your complaint regarding the error, the item typically cannot be included in a rapid rescoring process.

- They can't vow to support your score—"How Credit Scoring Works," sometimes removing negative items can really hurt a score—strange as that may appear.

The scoring formula attempts to contrast you with people who have comparable credit histories. In the event that you've been lumped into the gathering with a bankruptcy or other dark spots on your report, you may find that your score falls when a portion of those negative items are removed. Rather than being at the highest point of the bankrupts' gathering, as such, you've dropped to the base of the following gathering—the people who have better credit. All the more commonly, removing an error probably won't help your score as much as you may have trusted and probably won't win you a superior interest rate. There are no assurances with rapid rescoring.

Quite a long time ago, brokers and other lending professionals could take care of these problems. In the days prior to the widespread utilization of a credit score, a broker or loan officer could mediate to persuade a lender to disregard mistakes or little imperfections on a client's credit file. Everybody included comprehended that credit report errors were common, and having an accomplished loan pro vouch for your creditworthiness could frequently complete an arrangement.

With the coming of credit scoring and automated loan processes, however, those chances to advocate for clients quickly evaporated. Lending professionals shared consumers' dissatisfaction when incorrect information continued to be reported by the bureaus—information that frequently hosed credit scores and brought about more awful rates and terms than the borrower merited. The mortgage brokers needed an approach to slice through the bureaucracy and accelerate the process. Free credit reporting agencies, with their littler, specific staffs, started to fill the need. Here's the means by which it works. Your broker loan or officer obtains evidence from you that a mistake has been done, and he sends that proof to the credit agency that provides the rapid rescoring service.

The recorders, thusly, have uncommon associations with the credit bureaus that enable their requests to be handled quickly. The rescoring service transfers proof of errors to unique departments at the credit bureaus, and the departments contact the creditors (typically electronically). In the event that the creditor concurs that an error was made, the bureaus quickly update your credit report. After that occurs, another credit score can be calculated. The expense for this service is typically somewhere close to $50 and $100 for each "trade line" or account that is remedied, albeit a few agencies provide the rescoring for no additional charge, as part of a part of services provided to lending professionals.

The presence of rapid rescoring does not change the way that you should be proactive about your credit.

Months before applying for any loan, you have to order copies of your reports and start testing any errors. You likewise need to keep your correspondence about these errors. All things considered; rapid recorders typically require some kind of paper trail to pursue to prove to the bureau that the mistakes in fact exist. In any case, If that you wind up highly involved with getting a mortgage and an old problem repeats, rapid rescoring can assist you with disposing of the problem and spare the arrangement.

All in all, how would you discover one of these services? In case you're already managing a loan officer or mortgage broker, ask whether she approaches a rapid rescoring service. If that your lending pro has never known about rapid rescoring— it's an ongoing enough advancement that some haven't—request that her contact the agency that provides her organization with credit reports to check whether it's accessible.

Boosting Your Score in 30 to 60 Days

Rebuilding your credit can sometimes be an excruciatingly slow process, yet you can take a couple of easy routes that may increase your score in as meager as a month or two, as talked about in the accompanying segments.

Pay Off Your Lines of Credit & Credit Cards.

Probably the fastest approaches to support a score is to lower your debt use proportion—the distinction between the amounts of revolving credit that is accessible to you and the amount that you're utilizing. One straightforward approach to improve your proportion is to redistribute your debt. In the event that you have a big balance on one card, for instance, you could transfer probably a portion of the debt to different cards. It's usually better for your scores to have little balances on a number of cards than a big balance on a solitary card. You additionally could explore getting a personal installment loan with your nearby credit association or bank, and utilize the cash to pay down your cards. Applying for the loan may affect your scores a piece; however, that is probably going to be more than offset by the development to your scores from lessening the balances on your credit cards. (Credit scoring formulas are substantially more delicate to the balances on revolving debt, for example, credit cards, than to the balances on installment loans.)

Utilize Your Credit Cards Lightly

A big difference between your balances and your limits is what the scoring formula likes to see —and it doesn't really care whether you pay off your balances in full each month or carry them from month to month. What makes a difference is the amount of your credit limits you're really utilizing at some random time. A few people demand they've supported their scores by paying off their cards in full a couple of days before their announcement closes. In the event that their credit card backers, as a rule, send out bills around the 25th, for instance, these people check their balances online about seven days prior and pay off whatever's owed, in addition to a couple of bucks to cover any charges that may manifest before the 25th. When the bills are really printed, their balances are pretty close to zero. (In the event that you utilize this method, simply make sure you make a second payment after your announcement shows up if your balance isn't already zero. That will make sure you don't get damaged with late charges—and truly, that can occur, despite the fact that you made a payment before in the month.)

Concentrate on Correcting the Big Mistakes on Your Credit Reports

If that another person's bankruptcy, collections, or charge-offs are showing up on your report, you will probably profit by having those removed. If that an account you closed is reported as open, then again, you'll probably need to disregard it. Having an account filed as "closed" on your file can't support your score and may hurt it.

Utilize the Bureaus' Online Dispute Process

Some credit-fix veterans swear they get faster results along these lines, however regardless, you'll have to make printouts of all that you send to the bureaus and each correspondence you get from them.

Check whether You Can Have Your Creditors Update Positive Accounts or to Report

Not all creditors report to every one of the three bureaus, and some don't report reliably. If that you can get a creditor to report an account that is in good standing; however, you may see a quick knock in your score.

NOTE:

CPSIA information can be obtained
at www.ICGtesting.com
Printed in the USA
BVHW031523010822
643529BV00013B/257